Easy Sudoku
Puzzle Books For Kids
5-7 years

D1494734

What is Sudoku?

Sudoku is a puzzle that originated in Japan and to solve it the player must fill in all the missing numbers in a grid. Traditionally these grids are 9 squares across and 9 down but today there are many variations, including the 4 x 4 and 6 x 6 in this book.

How to play Sudoku

The 6 x 6 puzzle below consists of one large square containing 6 rows, 6 columns and 6 'blocks' of 6 smaller squares.

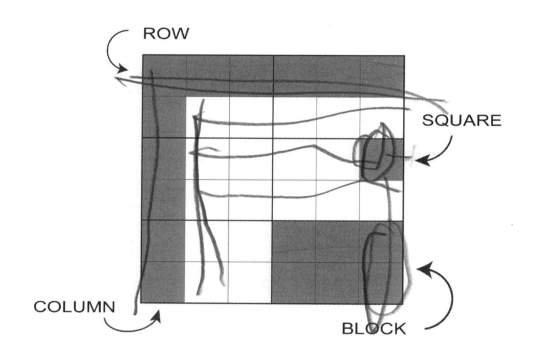

When playing a 6 x 6 puzzle each block, column and row must contain all the numbers 1, 2, 3, 4, 5, 6. This means they must also only occur once in each row, column, and block.

To discover which numbers are missing the player should start by looking across the rows, down the columns or in the blocks to see which numbers have already been given.

Try looking across the top row of this section of a 6 x 6 puzzle.

1	6		2	4	

Which numbers between 1 - 6 are missing? Easy isn't it?!
Ah…but which way round do they go? To discover the answer, we
need to reveal more of the puzzle.

1	6	5	2	4	3
		3		5	

We know that the missing numbers from our first row are 3 and
5. We can also see that there is already a 3 in the first block and
because numbers cannot be repeated in any column, row or block,
the 5 must go next to the 6 and the 3 next to the 4.

Like this…

1	6	5	2	4	3
		3		5	

Now you've completed the top row you can look for other missing
numbers.

Which numbers are missing from the top-left block and the top right
block? Have you worked it out? But, which way round do they go?
To find out, we need to look even further down the puzzle.

1	6	5	2	4	3
	\	3		5	
			1		
4					

If you look at the section of puzzle above, you will see there is already a 4 in the first column, this means a 4 cannot go under the 1 in the top left block and so it must go under the 6.

Try writing it in.

That leaves just one space left in the top left block, that's right, the 2! Now then, can you complete the top right block?

You have now solved part of the puzzle by a 'process of elimination'. This is key to solving Sudoku. To complete the full puzzle, all you need to do is to carry on eliminating!

To get you going, we've started you off with a set of 4 x 4 puzzles. If you find these too easy then why not try timing yourself! Can you beat your best time?

Good luck!

4x4 Puzzles

1

2	4	1	3
1	3	2	4
4	1	3	2
3	2	4	1

Time.......................

Time.......................

2

4	2	3	1
1	3	2	4
2	4	1	3
3	1	4	2

3

4	2	3	1
1	3	4	2
3	1	2	4
2	4	1	3

4

4	3	1	2
1	2	3	4
2	1	4	3
3	4	2	1

5

4	1	3	2
2	3	4	1
3	2	1	4
1	4	2	3

Time......................

Time......................

6

4	1	3	2
2	3	1	4
1	4	2	3
3	2	4	1

7

3	4	1	2
2	1	4	3
1	2	3	4
4	3	2	1

8

1	4	3	2
2	3	1	4
3	2	4	1
4	1	2	3

9

4	3	1	2
2	1	4	3
3	2	1	4
1	4	3	2

10

3	2	1	4
1	4	3	2
4	1	2	3
2	3	4	1

2	4	3	1
3	1	2	4
1	3	4	2
4	2	1	3

Time.......................

Time.......................

		4	
4	1	2	3
3	2	1	4
1			

13

1			2
		4	
	1		
3			4

14

	3		
2		3	1
3	2	1	4
4	1		

15

4		2	1
1	2	4	
	4		
2			4

16

2		1	
3		4	
1	2		4

17

		4	
	3		1
1			2
3			

18

		4	1
1	4		
4	3	1	2
2	1		

3			4
4	2		
1	4		2
	3		

Time......................

Time......................

	3		4
	2		3
	1	4	
	4		

21

1			2
		2	
	3	4	

22

2			
		1	
3	4		1
1		3	4

23

	3	1	
1			3
	4		
3	1	2	

24

2			1
4	1		
3	2	1	
		3	

25

3	4		2
1	2	4	3
4	3	2	1

Time.......................

26

4	3		2
		4	
3	4	2	
1	2		4

	4	2	1
2			
4	3		2
	2		4

Time........................

Time........................

4		3	1
1			
			3
		4	2

	2		
3	4		1
4	3		
2	1		3

Time......................

Time......................

4			
	3		
	2	4	1
1	4		3

	1	3	
	2		
1			3
	3	4	1

4			1
		3	
2	4	1	3
3			2

33

		1	4
		2	
1		3	
2	3	4	1

34

4			3
3	2		4
	4	3	
			1

35

3	4		
1			3
		2	1
	1	3	

Time........................

Time........................

36

3	1		4
			3
4	2		

	3		
2	1		4
	4	1	
1		4	3

1			4
4		2	1
		4	3
	4		2

	1	4	
3		1	
		2	4
	2	3	1

3		1	2
2			
	3	2	
		4	3

1		4	2
		3	
	1	2	3
3	2	1	

Time.......................

Time.......................

1			
	4	1	2
	1	2	3
2	3		

43

	1	2	4
			3
2		4	
1		3	

Time.......................

44

		3	4
4	3	2	
2			3
3		1	2

	3	1	
1	2	4	
3			1
2	1		4

Time......................

Time......................

4	1		3
2	3	1	4
3	2		

47

	4	3	
	2	4	1
	1		
2			4

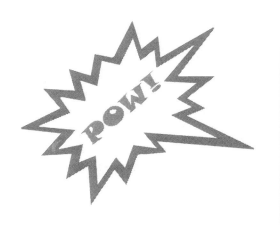

48

3		1	2
2			
	3	2	
		4	3

4		3	2
3	2	4	
2	3	1	
1			

	1	4	
	2		1
2	4	1	3
		2	

51

2			3
3	4	2	1
1		3	4
	3		

SUPER
HERO

52

3			
2	4		3
4			1
1	3	4	2

6x6 Puzzles

	3		1	6	
	4		3	5	2
3	2		4		5
4			6	2	
	5		2	4	6
2			5		1

3		6	1	2	
	1				
5	3				
			5	3	2
		3	2	4	1
	2	4	3		

Time........................

	6		5		
	1			2	6
4	5		1	3	2
1	3		6	5	4
		5		6	
6	2	1	3	4	

Time........................

		1		3	2
	6	3		1	
6	5	4	3	2	
1			4		
				2	
	2		1	4	

Time......................

	1			4	3
3					1
					6
4	6	3		2	5
6	5		3	1	
		1			4

Time......................

	4	1			5
2			4	1	
4		3	1	5	6
		4			1
6			5		4

5		3	4	1	
6		1	2		3
		4	5	3	2
2	3		6		1
	5	2			
		6		2	

Time........................

Time........................

		5	4		6
3	4				
5		4			3
1	6	3		4	
4	3		1		5
					4

5		6	3	4	
				6	2
2			1		6
	6				5
3		2			
6		4	2		

Time.......................

Time.......................

2	1		6	5	4
		4		2	3
		2	5	3	6
			4	1	2
	6	5			1
4	2			6	5

63

5	6			1	2
	2	1	6	5	4
	5	3			
	4	6	2		5
	3	5			
6	1		5	4	

Time......................

Time......................

64

	3				
1	6		4		5
		3	6	4	
	4	1	2	5	3
				5		6
5		6	3	2	

65

2	5	1		3	
	4	6			5
1	6		5		
5	2				1
	3	5			
	1			5	4

Time.........................

66

	3		6	2	5
	5				1
1	4		2	5	
	2	6		3	
2	1	5		6	3
			5	1	2

	4				
	6	2	4		3
2	3		1		5
	1	5		2	
		1	5		6
	5			4	1

Time...........................

Time........................

	1	3	5		6
		5		1	
3		1			5
5		6	1	3	4
		4			2
	5	2		4	1

	1	4		6	
3	6		4		1
	4	3	1		2
	2	1	3		
1	5		2		4
	3	2	6	1	

Time......................

Time......................

	2	5	3	4	
4					5
		3	4	6	1
6	1	4			3
		1			2
	6				4

	2		4	6	5
4	5	6	3		1
					6
6	4	5	2		3
		4		3	
2	3	1	6	5	

Time.........................

Time.........................

	4		5		3
			4	1	2
	5		6	2	1
	2		3		
	1	4		5	6
2	6	5		3	4

	1	6	3		4
	3	4	1		
3		5			2
		2	4		5
	2	1	5		
4			2	6	

Time......................

Time......................

		4			1
1	5	6		2	
		5	1		3
	1		2		6
			4	1	
5		1			2

	5	6		3	1
2		3		4	
	4			1	
1				5	4
			4		
5	2	4		6	3

Time.........................

Time.........................

	2			1	
3	1	5			
	5	3			
4				3	1
	3	6		5	4
			2		3

		5	2		
		6		5	
		4	1	2	
1	3	2		4	
				1	2
2			4	3	

Time......................

Time......................

1	5		2		6
6	2			4	
		5		1	
				2	4
		2	4		1
4	6			5	

2			4	1	
4	1		2	3	6
5	2	1	6		
		3	5		
1	6	4		5	
	5	2		6	4

Time.......................

Time.......................

5	1	2		3	
					5
			4	6	
		3	2	5	1
1	3	6	5	4	
4		5			6

81

			4	3	6
6		4	5		
4	2				5
3	6			1	4
2		6	1	5	
1		3			

Time........................

82

	3		4	5	1
	4	5	6		
		3		6	5
	5	6		3	4
5	2			1	6
		1	5		2

83

2		3	4	5	
4			3	2	6
		5			4
		4	1		
5	4		6		
		6			2

84

2					1
				2	
1	4		6	5	
5	2	6	3		4
3	6			4	5
4	1	5	2	3	

85

				6	4
4	2	6	5		
5		1	3		
	5	4	1	2	
3	1	2			6

86

Time.........................

	2		5	4	6
6	4	5	2	3	
				4	2
4		2	1	6	
2		3	6		4
			3		2

87

	4		2	5	
2					3
		4		2	1
1		5			4
	1	3		4	2
4	6	2	1		5

88

5			2		3
1	2	3	6		5
		1			
6					3
			1	2	6
	1			5	

		3		6	2
				4	5
		4	5	2	
		5		1	4
	4	1			6
3	2	6	4	5	

Time........................

Time........................

		1			3
3	2		6	1	
		6	5	3	2
	3			6	4
	4			2	6
	6			5	1

	1		5		4
4	5	3	6		2
5	3			2	
2	6	1	3		
		5		6	3
3	4			5	1

		5			
2	1				5
	5	2			1
1		3			
3		1		5	4
5		4			3

6		5	2		
	4	3	1	6	5
	6	1	4	2	
3					6
4	3		6	5	1
	5				2

Time........................

Time........................

		5	2	3	6
	2			4	
5				6	3
3	6		5		1
4			6	5	2

6	4	2	1		3
	5	1			4
2			4		
1	3	4		2	5
4	2				6
5	1		3	4	

Time......................

Time......................

1	5		6	4	2
6	2		5		
		5	4	2	6
		6	3		
4				6	5
		2	1		

	5	1	3	6	4
	3	6	2		
6	2	3	4		
1			6		
	6	4			

Time ....

Time ....

1				5	4
2	4		3	6	1
	5		4	2	6
		4			3
5	1			4	2
4		2	1	3	

		5	1	3	6
		3		2	5
1	5	2	3	6	
3			2	5	1
	2	6		1	3
				4	

5			6		1
			5	4	2
				6	3
1		6	4		
4	2		3		6
		3	2	5	4

101

	4	2			
5	3		2	6	
2		3	6	4	
1		4	3	5	
	1		4		
4	2	6	5	1	

Time......................

Time......................

102

2	1	3		4	5
4		6		1	3
6			5	3	
5			4		6
3	6		1		2
				6	

6	4	3	5	2	1
		5			
	6	2			
3	5		2		4
	3		1		2
		4		5	

Time........................

Time........................

3	4	1		6	
				4	
			6	2	
2		3		1	5
			1	3	
	3	6		5	4

	1			3	
3			6	1	
1		6	2	5	4
5			3		1
2		1	5	4	
				2	

Time......................

Time......................

6			4		2
	2		5		6
1	3	2	6	4	5
	6			2	
2			1	5	3
5		3		6	

107

		4	6		1
	1	2		3	4
		3			6
	6	1			
			4	1	5
	4			6	3

Time.......................

Time.......................

108

3		2			
6		4	3		
4	3	5	1	2	
2	6	1			3
		6	2	3	1

109

5	1				6
	4	6		3	
				6	1
				2	
	5	4	6	1	
	2	1		5	4

110

	3			2	1
1				5	6
	5			1	4
			5	3	
5	4	1		6	
3					

111

2			1	3	5
1	5	3		4	2
5		1	4	2	6
6	4		3		
		5			
	2	6	5	1	

Time ....

Time ....

112

5	1	2		6	
6	3		2	1	5
	4				
		3	4	2	
3	2	5			
				5	2

113

	2	6	5		1
	3	2		1	5
	5	4		2	6
4				3	
2	1	3			

114

3	1		6	2	5
			1		
4	3	5	2	1	6
2		1			
	4		5		2
		2	3		

4	5	2			
	1		4	2	
2			1	6	
1			5	4	2
			2	5	
5	2	4		3	

Time ....

SuperOWL

Time ....

5				2	
6	3		1	5	4
3				4	
	6	4	5		
	2	3			
	5			3	1

117

3		1		2	4
2	4	5	6		1
	3		1	5	
	1	6		4	
1	2	4			
	5		4	1	2

Time.......................

118

2					
4				1	2
5	4		2	3	6
3	6		4	5	
6	3	4			
		5	3		4

3	6	2	5	4	
1			3		2
6	3				4
2	4		6	3	
		3	1		
	1				

Time ....

Time ....

5		4	2		
2	3	1			6
3		6			2
	4	2		3	5
4			3	6	
					4

121

4	5	6	1		2
2		1	6	5	4
5	1	2			
6	4	3			
	6		2		
	2		3	4	6

122

2			3		
4	6	3	1		
	5			4	
		2	6		
	3	4	5		
5	2	6	4	3	

1	3	5	6	4	
4	2	6	1		
5				3	
3	6		4		
6	4	3		2	
	5		3	6	4

Time........................

Time........................

				6	
3	2	6	4		
5				2	
2					4
6	1		5		2
4		2	1		6

3					6
4	5	6	3		
		4	2		5
		5	1		
6	1		5	2	
	4	2	6	3	

Time......................

Time......................

			3		
		1			2
	6		2	3	5
2	5		4		6
4	1				3
		6	1	2	

	5		6	2	1
	2				
6	3	5		1	
	1			5	
5	6		2		
	4	2		6	5

Time.........................

Time.........................

		4	1		
5					
3	5	2			
	1	6	3	5	
		3	5		4
2			6		3

2			6	4	

129

2				6	4
3	6		5		1
5			1	3	2
1				4	
		3		5	
				1	3

Time........................

Time........................

2			6	5	3
		3		1	4
3		5		6	
	1	4	5	3	
	5		3		6
4	3			2	5

131

4	1		5	3	
2		3	4		1
3		4			5
	2	1			
1	4			5	6
	3		2		

132

		5			4
			1	6	
2	3		5	1	6
6					3
		6	4		2
5	4		6	3	

133

	3		4	5	
	2	5			
4		3	2		5
2	5	1		4	
3		4	5	2	

Time......................

Time......................

134

3	2		6	4	
6			5	2	
		2	1		6
		6	2	5	
5	6	4	3		2
	1		4	6	

	4		2		1
1	2	5			
2	5	1		4	
6	3	4			2
		3	1	2	
	1	2	4	6	

Time........................

Time........................

4		3		5	6
5	2			3	1
3	4			6	2
	5	2	1		
1	3	4	6		5
				1	4

	3				5
			4	3	6
4	5				2
1	2		5	4	
		5	6	2	
2		1		5	4

Time ....

Time ....

1			2		
	4	6	5		
6				5	
	3	1		2	
4	1		6	3	2
3	6	2			5

1		5	6	3	
	3				
4	5		3	2	
3	6			4	1
6		3	1	5	4
5	1	4	2		

6				2	4
4	2				6
				1	2
1		2	3		
2	1		4		3
	4			6	

	5	4	6		
	3	6	4	5	
		5		4	
		2	5		
	2				4
4		3			5

3				2	
6	2		5	3	
	4	5	2		3
2				5	
			3		
	3	2		1	5

2		4	3	6	
3	6	1	5	4	
6	1		2	3	
4			6	1	
1				5	6
5				2	3

Time.........................

Time.........................

			2		1
		1		3	5
	1	4	5	6	3
6		3			2
3			1	2	
	6	2	3	5	4

	5		4	1	3
1			5	6	
5					
	6	1	3		
	1	5		3	
			1	5	6

Time........................

Time.......................

5	6	4	3		2
1					5
4	5				1
		1	5	6	
	1	5	4		3
3		2		5	6

147

			3		4
3	4	1		5	6
			4	6	
4	1			2	
5		4	1		2
					5

148

1	2				
6					2
		6	2	4	1
4	1		6		5
	4		1		3
3		1	5		

Time........................

Time........................

Puzzle 149:

1		3		4	6
2		1	6	5	4
6		5	3		1
		4	2		3
3	6				

Puzzle 150:

2	3		4		6
4				1	2
3	1	4			
		5		3	
5	4	3	6		
	6	2	5	4	3

			3	5	
6	3	5		4	2
5		3	6	1	
4			2		
		6			
3	5	2			

Time.......................

Time.......................

	1	6			
4	3	2		5	
		5	1		2
		1		6	5
1	5			4	
2		4		1	3

1		3		5	2
4		2	6		3
	1	6	5	2	4
2			1	3	6
5		4	2	6	

Time........................

Time........................

				2	1
4	1		3		
2			6		3
	6		5	4	
	5	1		6	4
	2			3	5

155

				3	6
3			1		4
4	1	6	2	5	3
1					2
	2	4		1	

156

3		5		2	4
2	1	4		6	3
	3	2	6		
	5	6			2
5		3			6
6					

Solutions

1

2	4	1	3
1	3	2	4
4	1	3	2
3	2	4	1

2

4	2	3	1
1	3	2	4
2	4	1	3
3	1	4	2

3

4	2	3	1
1	3	4	2
3	1	2	4
2	4	1	3

4

4	3	1	2
1	2	3	4
2	1	4	3
3	4	2	1

5

4	1	3	2
2	3	4	1
3	2	1	4
1	4	2	3

6

4	1	3	2
2	3	1	4
1	4	2	3
3	2	4	1

7

3	4	1	2
2	1	4	3
1	2	3	4
4	3	2	1

8

1	4	3	2
2	3	1	4
3	2	4	1
4	1	2	3

9

4	3	1	2
2	1	4	3
3	4	2	1
1	2	3	4

10

3	2	1	4
1	4	3	2
4	1	2	3
2	3	4	1

11

2	4	3	1
3	1	2	4
1	3	4	2
4	2	1	3

12

2	3	4	1
4	1	2	3
3	2	1	4
1	4	3	2

13

1	4	3	2
2	3	4	1
4	1	2	3
3	2	1	4

14

1	3	4	2
2	4	3	1
3	2	1	4
4	1	2	3

15

4	3	2	1
1	2	4	3
3	4	1	2
2	1	3	4

16

2	4	1	3
3	1	4	2
4	3	2	1
1	2	3	4

17

2	1	4	3
4	3	2	1
1	4	3	2
3	2	1	4

18

3	2	4	1
1	4	2	3
4	3	1	2
2	1	3	4

19

3	1	2	4
4	2	1	3
1	4	3	2
2	3	4	1

20

1	3	2	4
4	2	1	3
3	1	4	2
2	4	3	1

21

1	4	3	2
3	2	1	4
4	1	2	3
2	3	4	1

22

2	1	4	3
4	3	1	2
3	4	2	1
1	2	3	4

23

4	3	1	2
1	2	4	3
2	4	3	1
3	1	2	4

24

2	3	4	1
4	1	2	3
3	2	1	4
1	4	3	2

25

3	4	1	2
2	1	3	4
1	2	4	3
4	3	2	1

26

4	3	1	2
2	1	4	3
3	4	2	1
1	2	3	4

27

3	4	2	1
2	1	4	3
4	3	1	2
1	2	3	4

28

4	2	3	1
1	3	2	4
2	4	1	3
3	1	4	2

29

1	2	3	4
3	4	2	1
4	3	1	2
2	1	4	3

30

4	1	3	2
2	3	1	4
3	2	4	1
1	4	2	3

31

4	1	3	2
3	2	1	4
1	4	2	3
2	3	4	1

32

4	3	2	1
1	2	3	4
2	4	1	3
3	1	4	2

33

3	2	1	4
4	1	2	3
1	4	3	2
2	3	4	1

34

4	1	2	3
3	2	1	4
1	4	3	2
2	3	4	1

35

3	4	1	2
1	2	4	3
4	3	2	1
2	1	3	4

36

3	1	2	4
2	4	1	3
1	3	4	2
4	2	3	1

37

4	3	2	1
2	1	3	4
3	4	1	2
1	2	4	3

38

1	2	3	4
4	3	2	1
2	1	4	3
3	4	1	2

39

2	1	4	3
3	4	1	2
1	3	2	4
4	2	3	1

40

3	4	1	2
2	1	3	4
4	3	2	1
1	2	4	3

41

1	3	4	2
2	4	3	1
4	1	2	3
3	2	1	4

42

1	2	3	4
3	4	1	2
4	1	2	3
2	3	4	1

43

3	1	2	4
4	2	1	3
2	3	4	1
1	4	3	2

44

1	2	3	4
4	3	2	1
2	1	4	3
3	4	1	2

45

4	3	1	2
1	2	4	3
3	4	2	1
2	1	3	4

46

4	1	2	3
2	3	1	4
1	4	3	2
3	2	4	1

47

1	4	3	2
3	2	4	1
4	1	2	3
2	3	1	4

48

3	4	1	2
2	1	3	4
4	3	2	1
1	2	4	3

49

4	1	3	2
3	2	4	1
2	3	1	4
1	4	2	3

50

3	1	4	2
4	2	3	1
2	4	1	3
1	3	2	4

51

2	1	4	3
3	4	2	1
1	2	3	4
4	3	1	2

52

3	1	2	4
2	4	1	3
4	2	3	1
1	3	4	2

53

5	3	2	1	6	4
6	4	1	3	5	2
3	2	6	4	1	5
4	1	5	6	2	3
1	5	3	2	4	6
2	6	4	5	3	1

54

3	4	6	1	2	5
2	1	5	4	6	3
5	3	2	6	1	4
4	6	1	5	3	2
6	5	3	2	4	1
1	2	4	3	5	6

55

2	6	4	5	1	3
5	1	3	4	2	6
4	5	6	1	3	2
1	3	2	6	5	4
3	4	5	2	6	1
6	2	1	3	4	5

56

5	4	1	6	3	2
2	6	3	5	1	4
6	5	4	3	2	1
1	3	2	4	6	5
4	1	6	2	5	3
3	2	5	1	4	6

57

5	1	6	2	4	3
3	4	2	6	5	1
1	2	5	4	3	6
4	6	3	1	2	5
6	5	4	3	1	2
2	3	1	5	6	4

58

3	4	1	6	2	5
2	5	6	4	1	3
4	2	3	1	5	6
1	6	5	3	4	2
5	3	4	2	6	1
6	1	2	5	3	4

59

5	2	3	4	1	6
6	4	1	2	5	3
1	6	4	5	3	2
2	3	5	6	4	1
3	5	2	1	6	4
4	1	6	3	2	5

60

2	1	5	4	3	6
3	4	6	2	5	1
5	2	4	6	1	3
1	6	3	5	4	2
4	3	2	1	6	5
6	5	1	3	2	4

61

5	2	6	3	4	1
4	3	1	6	5	2
2	4	5	1	3	6
1	6	3	4	2	5
3	1	2	5	6	4
6	5	4	2	1	3

62

2	1	3	6	5	4
6	5	4	1	2	3
1	4	2	5	3	6
5	3	6	4	1	2
3	6	5	2	4	1
4	2	1	3	6	5

63

5	6	4	3	1	2
3	2	1	6	5	4
2	5	3	4	6	1
1	4	6	2	3	5
4	3	5	1	2	6
6	1	2	5	4	3

64

4	3	5	1	6	2
1	6	2	4	3	5
2	5	3	6	4	1
6	4	1	2	5	3
3	2	4	5	1	6
5	1	6	3	2	4

65

2	5	1	4	3	6
3	4	6	2	1	5
1	6	4	5	2	3
5	2	3	6	4	1
4	3	5	1	6	2
6	1	2	3	5	4

66

4	3	1	6	2	5
6	5	2	3	4	1
1	4	3	2	5	6
5	2	6	1	3	4
2	1	5	4	6	3
3	6	4	5	1	2

67

1	4	3	6	5	2
5	6	2	4	1	3
2	3	4	1	6	5
6	1	5	3	2	4
4	2	1	5	3	6
3	5	6	2	4	1

68

4	1	3	5	2	6
2	6	5	4	1	3
3	4	1	2	6	5
5	2	6	1	3	4
1	3	4	6	5	2
6	5	2	3	4	1

69

2	1	4	5	6	3
3	6	5	4	2	1
6	4	3	1	5	2
5	2	1	3	4	6
1	5	6	2	3	4
4	3	2	6	1	5

70

1	2	5	3	4	6
4	3	6	2	1	5
2	5	3	4	6	1
6	1	4	5	2	3
3	4	1	6	5	2
5	6	2	1	3	4

71

1	2	3	4	6	5
4	5	6	3	2	1
3	1	2	5	4	6
6	4	5	2	1	3
5	6	4	1	3	2
2	3	1	6	5	4

72

1	4	2	5	6	3
5	3	6	4	1	2
4	5	3	6	2	1
6	2	1	3	4	5
3	1	4	2	5	6
2	6	5	1	3	4

73

5	1	6	3	2	4
2	3	4	1	5	6
3	4	5	6	1	2
1	6	2	4	3	5
6	2	1	5	4	3
4	5	3	2	6	1

74

2	3	4	5	6	1
1	5	6	3	2	4
6	2	5	1	4	3
4	1	3	2	5	6
3	6	2	4	1	5
5	4	1	6	3	2

75

4	5	6	2	3	1
2	1	3	5	4	6
6	4	5	3	1	2
1	3	2	6	5	4
3	6	1	4	2	5
5	2	4	1	6	3

76

6	2	4	3	1	5
3	1	5	6	4	2
1	5	3	4	2	6
4	6	2	5	3	1
2	3	6	1	5	4
5	4	1	2	6	3

77

3	1	5	2	6	4
4	2	6	3	5	1
5	6	4	1	2	3
1	3	2	6	4	5
6	4	3	5	1	2
2	5	1	4	3	6

78

1	5	4	2	3	6
6	2	3	1	4	5
2	4	5	6	1	3
3	1	6	5	2	4
5	3	2	4	6	1
4	6	1	3	5	2

79

2	3	6	4	1	5
4	1	5	2	3	6
5	2	1	6	4	3
6	4	3	5	2	1
1	6	4	3	5	2
3	5	2	1	6	4

80

5	1	2	6	3	4
3	6	4	1	2	5
2	5	1	4	6	3
6	4	3	2	5	1
1	3	6	5	4	2
4	2	5	3	1	6

81

5	1	2	4	3	6
6	3	4	5	2	1
4	2	1	3	6	5
3	6	5	2	1	4
2	4	6	1	5	3
1	5	3	6	4	2

82

6	3	2	4	5	1
1	4	5	6	2	3
4	1	3	2	6	5
2	5	6	1	3	4
5	2	4	3	1	6
3	6	1	5	4	2

83

2	6	3	4	5	1
4	5	1	3	2	6
1	3	5	2	6	4
6	2	4	1	3	5
5	4	2	6	1	3
3	1	6	5	4	2

84

2	3	4	5	6	1
6	5	1	4	2	3
1	4	3	6	5	2
5	2	6	3	1	4
3	6	2	1	4	5
4	1	5	2	3	6

85

1	3	5	2	6	4
4	2	6	5	3	1
5	6	1	3	4	2
2	4	3	6	1	5
6	5	4	1	2	3
3	1	2	4	5	6

86

3	2	1	5	4	6
6	4	5	2	3	1
1	5	6	4	2	3
4	3	2	1	6	5
2	1	3	6	5	4
5	6	4	3	1	2

87

3	4	1	2	5	6
2	5	6	4	1	3
6	3	4	5	2	1
1	2	5	3	6	4
5	1	3	6	4	2
4	6	2	1	3	5

88

5	6	4	2	1	3
1	2	3	6	4	5
4	3	1	5	6	2
6	5	2	4	3	1
3	4	5	1	2	6
2	1	6	3	5	4

89

4	5	3	1	6	2
1	6	2	3	4	5
6	1	4	5	2	3
2	3	5	6	1	4
5	4	1	2	3	6
3	2	6	4	5	1

90

6	5	1	2	4	3
3	2	4	6	1	5
4	1	6	5	3	2
5	3	2	1	6	4
1	4	5	3	2	6
2	6	3	4	5	1

91

6	1	2	5	3	4
4	5	3	6	1	2
5	3	4	1	2	6
2	6	1	3	4	5
1	2	5	4	6	3
3	4	6	2	5	1

92

4	3	5	1	6	2
2	1	6	3	4	5
6	5	2	4	3	1
1	4	3	5	2	6
3	2	1	6	5	4
5	6	4	2	1	3

93

6	1	5	2	3	4
2	4	3	1	6	5
5	6	1	4	2	3
3	2	4	5	1	6
4	3	2	6	5	1
1	5	6	3	4	2

94

1	4	5	2	3	6
6	2	3	1	4	5
5	1	2	4	6	3
3	6	4	5	2	1
4	3	1	6	5	2
2	5	6	3	1	4

95

6	4	2	1	5	3
3	5	1	2	6	4
2	6	5	4	3	1
1	3	4	6	2	5
4	2	3	5	1	6
5	1	6	3	4	2

96

1	5	3	6	4	2
6	2	4	5	1	3
3	1	5	4	2	6
2	4	6	3	5	1
4	3	1	2	6	5
5	6	2	1	3	4

97

2	5	1	3	6	4
4	3	6	2	5	1
6	2	3	4	1	5
1	4	5	6	2	3
3	1	2	5	4	6
5	6	4	1	3	2

98

1	3	6	2	5	4
2	4	5	3	6	1
3	5	1	4	2	6
6	2	4	5	1	3
5	1	3	6	4	2
4	6	2	1	3	5

99

2	4	5	1	3	6
6	1	3	4	2	5
1	5	2	3	6	4
3	6	4	2	5	1
4	2	6	5	1	3
5	3	1	6	4	2

100

5	4	2	6	3	1
3	6	1	5	4	2
2	5	4	1	6	3
1	3	6	4	2	5
4	2	5	3	1	6
6	1	3	2	5	4

101

6	4	2	1	3	5
5	3	1	2	6	4
2	5	3	6	4	1
1	6	4	3	5	2
3	1	5	4	2	6
4	2	6	5	1	3

102

2	1	3	6	4	5
4	5	6	2	1	3
6	4	2	5	3	1
5	3	1	4	2	6
3	6	4	1	5	2
1	2	5	3	6	4

103

6	4	3	5	2	1
2	1	5	4	3	6
4	6	2	3	1	5
3	5	1	2	6	4
5	3	6	1	4	2
1	2	4	6	5	3

104

3	4	1	5	6	2
6	2	5	3	4	1
5	1	4	6	2	3
2	6	3	4	1	5
4	5	2	1	3	6
1	3	6	2	5	4

105

6	1	2	4	3	5
3	4	5	6	1	2
1	3	6	2	5	4
5	2	4	3	6	1
2	6	1	5	4	3
4	5	3	1	2	6

106

6	5	1	4	3	2
3	2	4	5	1	6
1	3	2	6	4	5
4	6	5	3	2	1
2	4	6	1	5	3
5	1	3	2	6	4

107

3	5	4	6	2	1
6	1	2	5	3	4
5	2	3	1	4	6
4	6	1	3	5	2
2	3	6	4	1	5
1	4	5	2	6	3

108

3	1	2	4	6	5
6	5	4	3	1	2
4	3	5	1	2	6
2	6	1	5	4	3
1	2	3	6	5	4
5	4	6	2	3	1

109

5	1	3	2	4	6
2	4	6	1	3	5
4	3	2	5	6	1
1	6	5	4	2	3
3	5	4	6	1	2
6	2	1	3	5	4

110

6	3	5	4	2	1
1	2	4	3	5	6
2	5	3	6	1	4
4	1	6	5	3	2
5	4	1	2	6	3
3	6	2	1	4	5

111

2	6	4	1	3	5
1	5	3	6	4	2
5	3	1	4	2	6
6	4	2	3	5	1
3	1	5	2	6	4
4	2	6	5	1	3

112

5	1	2	3	6	4
6	3	4	2	1	5
2	4	6	1	5	3
1	5	3	4	2	6
3	2	5	6	4	1
4	6	1	5	3	2

113

5	4	1	2	6	3
3	2	6	5	4	1
6	3	2	4	1	5
1	5	4	3	2	6
4	6	5	1	3	2
2	1	3	6	5	4

114

3	1	4	6	2	5
5	2	6	1	3	4
4	3	5	2	1	6
2	6	1	4	5	3
1	4	3	5	6	2
6	5	2	3	4	1

115

4	5	2	3	1	6
6	1	3	4	2	5
2	4	5	1	6	3
1	3	6	5	4	2
3	6	1	2	5	4
5	2	4	6	3	1

116

5	4	1	3	2	6
6	3	2	1	5	4
3	1	5	6	4	2
2	6	4	5	1	3
1	2	3	4	6	5
4	5	6	2	3	1

117

3	6	1	5	2	4
2	4	5	6	3	1
4	3	2	1	5	6
5	1	6	2	4	3
1	2	4	3	6	5
6	5	3	4	1	2

118

2	1	6	5	4	3
4	5	3	6	1	2
5	4	1	2	3	6
3	6	2	4	5	1
6	3	4	1	2	5
1	2	5	3	6	4

119

3	6	2	5	4	1
1	5	4	3	6	2
6	3	5	2	1	4
2	4	1	6	3	5
4	2	3	1	5	6
5	1	6	4	2	3

120

5	6	4	2	1	3
2	3	1	4	5	6
3	5	6	1	4	2
1	4	2	6	3	5
4	2	5	3	6	1
6	1	3	5	2	4

121

4	5	6	1	3	2
2	3	1	6	5	4
5	1	2	4	6	3
6	4	3	5	2	1
3	6	4	2	1	5
1	2	5	3	4	6

122

2	1	5	3	6	4
4	6	3	1	5	2
6	5	1	2	4	3
3	4	2	6	1	5
1	3	4	5	2	6
5	2	6	4	3	1

123

1	3	5	6	4	2
4	2	6	1	5	3
5	1	4	2	3	6
3	6	2	4	1	5
6	4	3	5	2	1
2	5	1	3	6	4

124

1	4	5	2	6	3
3	2	6	4	1	5
5	6	4	3	2	1
2	3	1	6	5	4
6	1	3	5	4	2
4	5	2	1	3	6

125

3	2	1	4	5	6
4	5	6	3	1	2
1	3	4	2	6	5
2	6	5	1	4	3
6	1	3	5	2	4
5	4	2	6	3	1

126

6	2	5	3	4	1
3	4	1	5	6	2
1	6	4	2	3	5
2	5	3	4	1	6
4	1	2	6	5	3
5	3	6	1	2	4

127

4	5	3	6	2	1
1	2	6	5	4	3
6	3	5	4	1	2
2	1	4	3	5	6
5	6	1	2	3	4
3	4	2	1	6	5

128

6	2	4	1	3	5
5	3	1	2	4	6
3	5	2	4	6	1
4	1	6	3	5	2
1	6	3	5	2	4
2	4	5	6	1	3

129

2	5	1	3	6	4
3	6	4	5	2	1
5	4	6	1	3	2
1	3	2	6	4	5
4	1	3	2	5	6
6	2	5	4	1	3

130

2	4	1	6	5	3
5	6	3	2	1	4
3	2	5	4	6	1
6	1	4	5	3	2
1	5	2	3	4	6
4	3	6	1	2	5

131

4	1	6	5	3	2
2	5	3	4	6	1
3	6	4	1	2	5
5	2	1	6	4	3
1	4	2	3	5	6
6	3	5	2	1	4

132

1	6	5	3	2	4
4	2	3	1	6	5
2	3	4	5	1	6
6	5	1	2	4	3
3	1	6	4	5	2
5	4	2	6	3	1

133

5	4	2	1	3	6
1	3	6	4	5	2
6	2	5	3	1	4
4	1	3	2	6	5
2	5	1	6	4	3
3	6	4	5	2	1

134

3	2	5	6	4	1
6	4	1	5	2	3
4	5	2	1	3	6
1	3	6	2	5	4
5	6	4	3	1	2
2	1	3	4	6	5

135

3	4	6	2	5	1
1	2	5	6	3	4
2	5	1	3	4	6
6	3	4	5	1	2
4	6	3	1	2	5
5	1	2	4	6	3

136

4	1	3	2	5	6
5	2	6	4	3	1
3	4	1	5	6	2
6	5	2	1	4	3
1	3	4	6	2	5
2	6	5	3	1	4

137

6	3	4	2	1	5
5	1	2	4	3	6
4	5	3	1	6	2
1	2	6	5	4	3
3	4	5	6	2	1
2	6	1	3	5	4

138

1	5	3	2	6	4
2	4	6	5	1	3
6	2	4	3	5	1
5	3	1	4	2	6
4	1	5	6	3	2
3	6	2	1	4	5

139

1	4	5	6	3	2
2	3	6	4	1	5
4	5	1	3	2	6
3	6	2	5	4	1
6	2	3	1	5	4
5	1	4	2	6	3

140

6	3	1	5	2	4
4	2	5	1	3	6
3	5	4	6	1	2
1	6	2	3	4	5
2	1	6	4	5	3
5	4	3	2	6	1

141

2	5	4	6	1	3
1	3	6	4	5	2
3	1	5	2	4	6
6	4	2	5	3	1
5	2	1	3	6	4
4	6	3	1	2	5

142

3	5	1	4	2	6
6	2	4	5	3	1
1	4	5	2	6	3
2	6	3	1	5	4
5	1	6	3	4	2
4	3	2	6	1	5

143

2	5	4	3	6	1
3	6	1	5	4	2
6	1	5	2	3	4
4	2	3	6	1	5
1	3	2	4	5	6
5	4	6	1	2	3

144

5	3	6	2	4	1
4	2	1	6	3	5
2	1	4	5	6	3
6	5	3	4	1	2
3	4	5	1	2	6
1	6	2	3	5	4

145

2	5	6	4	1	3
1	3	4	5	6	2
5	2	3	6	4	1
4	6	1	3	2	5
6	1	5	2	3	4
3	4	2	1	5	6

146

5	6	4	3	1	2
1	2	3	6	4	5
4	5	6	2	3	1
2	3	1	5	6	4
6	1	5	4	2	3
3	4	2	1	5	6

147

6	5	2	3	1	4
3	4	1	2	5	6
2	3	5	4	6	1
4	1	6	5	2	3
5	6	4	1	3	2
1	2	3	6	4	5

148

1	2	4	3	5	6
6	5	3	4	1	2
5	3	6	2	4	1
4	1	2	6	3	5
2	4	5	1	6	3
3	6	1	5	2	4

149

4	5	6	1	3	2
1	2	3	5	4	6
2	3	1	6	5	4
6	4	5	3	2	1
5	1	4	2	6	3
3	6	2	4	1	5

150

2	3	1	4	5	6
4	5	6	3	1	2
3	1	4	2	6	5
6	2	5	1	3	4
5	4	3	6	2	1
1	6	2	5	4	3

151

2	1	4	3	5	6
6	3	5	1	4	2
5	2	3	6	1	4
4	6	1	2	3	5
1	4	6	5	2	3
3	5	2	4	6	1

152

5	1	6	3	2	4
4	3	2	6	5	1
6	4	5	1	3	2
3	2	1	4	6	5
1	5	3	2	4	6
2	6	4	5	1	3

153

1	6	3	4	5	2
4	5	2	6	1	3
3	1	6	5	2	4
2	4	5	1	3	6
5	3	4	2	6	1
6	2	1	3	4	5

154

5	3	6	4	2	1
4	1	2	3	5	6
2	4	5	6	1	3
1	6	3	5	4	2
3	5	1	2	6	4
6	2	4	1	3	5

155

2	4	1	5	3	6
5	6	3	4	2	1
3	5	2	1	6	4
4	1	6	2	5	3
1	3	5	6	4	2
6	2	4	3	1	5

156

3	6	5	1	2	4
2	1	4	5	6	3
4	3	2	6	5	1
1	5	6	4	3	2
5	4	3	2	1	6
6	2	1	3	4	5

Thank you
for purchasing one
of our activity books!

If you enjoyed this book please leave an Amazon review using the QR links below.

And please let us know what you thought of our Sudoku puzzles on Instagram!

@KidWizardPress

THANK YOU!

www.KidWizardPress.com